OUTDOOR LIVING™

KAYAKING

SERENA J. THOMAS AND ALLISON STARK DRAPER

ROSEN
PUBLISHING

NEW YORK

Published in 2016 by The Rosen Publishing Group, Inc.
29 East 21st Street, New York, NY 10010

Library of Congress Cataloging-in-Publication Data

Thomas, Serena J.
   Kayaking / Serena J. Thomas and Allison Stark Draper. — First Edition.
      pages cm. — (Outdoor living)
   Includes bibliographical references and index.
   Audience: Grades: 7-12.
   ISBN 978-1-4994-6233-3 (Library bound)
   1. Kayaking—Juvenile literature. I. Draper, Allison Stark. II. Title.
   GV784.3.T45 2016
   797.122'4—dc23
                                    2015025481

Manufactured in China

CONTENTS

INTRODUCTION

Imagine being surrounded by the majestic heights of the Grand Canyon as you shoot down a fast-moving rapid on the Colorado River. Or perhaps you might be more comfortable taking in lush forests and colorful wildlife as you gently paddle through the Everglades. Whether you're an adventurous thrill-seeker, a casual sightseer, or somewhere in between, kayaking is an exciting way to experience a new place—or even a familiar place in a new way.

Kayaks were developed in ancient times—about eight or nine thousand years ago—by Inuit peoples of the Arctic to navigate difficult seas and narrow waterways effectively. Ancient kayaks were generally long boats, pointed at both ends, designed to hold one person who would use a double-bladed paddle to steer.

Modern kayaks include some of the same features, although there have been changes in the material and design. Kayaking has also transformed from a survival tool into a popular recreational activity that allows people all over the world to enjoy the outdoors. It can be done alone or in a group, on serene waterways or in whitewater rapids. Basic kayaking requires relatively little equipment and training, which means individuals of all ages can take it up at any time and get paddling fairly quickly.

Kayaking might be an ancient form of transportation, but it continues to appeal to new generations of adventurers and non-adventurers alike. After learning the equipment and some basic techniques, you, too, can take to the water. Whether you decide to work your way up to tackling rapids and vertical falls or stick to calmer waters on a lake or ocean, kayaking is sure to prove an enjoyable and rewarding experience.

You don't have to be a pro to enjoy kayaking. Kayaking is a great source of fun and exercise for people of all ages.

CHAPTER 1

THE HISTORY OF KAYAKING

The waters of the Arctic—which contain large expanses of ice sheets and where cold black inlets separate barren points of land—can be difficult to navigate. Kayaks are one type of canoe developed by the Inuit and Aleut peoples of Greenland and northern Canada to help them brave these sometimes treacherous areas. These narrow boats had a pointed bow and stern and were generally designed to seat one person who fit into a hole in the deck that was covered by animal skin. The design of these kayaks made them simple to maneuver and allowed a rider to more easily return to an upright position after capsizing, or tipping over. The covered deck would both insulate the rider from the cold and keep out the icy water. Double-bladed paddles helped kayakers steer.

For thousands of years, the Inuit peoples of Greenland and northern Canada have used kayaks to hunt. In fact, "kayak" means "hunter's boat." Because Arctic weather is bitter—the summers are

This man is paddling a traditional Inuit kayak made of seal skin. Although there are modern kayaks now, practicing traditional Inuit kayaking is becoming increasingly popular.

short, and the land is poor—the Inuit hunted animals for fur and meat rather than grow and harvest crops. The Inuit used their kayaks to hunt caribou, waterfowl, sea otter, and seal. It is difficult for a slow human to surprise these animals on foot or chase them into the sea. In a swift and silent kayak, however, a hunter could sneak up on an animal and kill it with a kind of spear called a harpoon.

Until the middle of the twentieth century, kayaks were essential to the survival of the Inuit. A hunter had to own a kayak and know how to use it before he could marry and start a family. Kayaks were so important that they were treated with almost religious respect. Each kayak was custom-made for one hunter.

KAYAK DESIGN

There are many types of kayaks, but they are all alike in certain ways. They are long (8 to 30 feet [2.5 to 9 meters]), narrow (1.5 to 3 feet [.5 to 1 m]), and shallow (9 inches to 2 feet [22 to 61 centimeters]). They have pointed ends and watertight, covered decks. In the center of the kayak, between the decks, is a hole slightly larger than the kayaker's waist. Kayakers enter their boats by sliding their legs into the hole and (unlike canoers, who kneel) stretching them out under the forward deck as they sit down. Kayaks do not have keels (the spine that runs along the bottom of the boat), so they turn easily, and they are extremely lightweight. Most Inuit kayaks were so light that hunters could carry their boats on their heads. This meant they could cross the ice out to the open water or walk overland from one inlet to another carrying their kayaks.

In addition to being light and fast, kayaks had to be strong enough to handle heavy Arctic seas. There were few big trees in the far north, so boat builders often used driftwood found on beaches to make kayak frames. To make a kayak, the builders first constructed the frame for the deck. They also used whalebone. Then they scraped seal or caribou hides completely clean of hair to make the hull. The hides were spread tightly over the frame. Rubbing animal fat over the hides helped make the kayak waterproof. If a kayak was regularly used in the extreme cold of the Arctic, the skin had to be oiled every four to eight days and changed entirely every year or two. Sometimes, in order to help the kayak float better, the Inuit would place seal bladders full of air in the front and back of the boat. The kayaks of different tribes of Inuit peoples varied according to use.

This is an example of a wooden frame used in the building of a traditional Inuit kayak. Other frames were made with whalebone.

Inuit kayakers generally used two paddle blades joined by one narrow shaft to paddle their boats. The blades of the paddle are on the same plane (or unfeathered). This design put less strain on paddlers' hands, wrists, and muscles, which was important because they often spent many hours in their kayaks. They paddled with a continuous, figure-eight arm motion. This was much faster than switching from side to side with a single paddle. It also gave them better control when they wanted to roll their kayaks.

Traditional Inuit kayak paddles are narrow and made of wood. Their light design helped Inuit hunters paddle for long stretches of time without tiring.

OTHER ANCIENT BOATS OF THE ARCTIC

Kayaks share much in common with canoes and umiaks, two other types of boats used by the Inuit. Kayaks and umiaks are actually both types of canoes. All require a paddle and have a similar design—a covered frame of wood or bone. The frames of kayaks and umiaks were usually covered by animal skin, while the frames of canoes were covered by wood or bark.

However, there are some notable differences. Traditional canoes and umiaks are open, while kayaks have a covered deck. Kayakers sit in an opening in this covering, with their legs outstretched, and steer, while riders in canoes and umiaks sit on an open seat or kneel. Canoes and umiaks can also carry more people. While there were kayaks built to hold two to three people, generally kayaks were reserved for one person (usually a male) to use in hunting or fishing. Umiaks were more often used as general transport by women for their families and belongings.

Umiaks have generally fallen out of use today, but canoeing and kayaking remain popular activities, even though modern advances have changed how they are used and made.

CAPSIZING

Rolling is when a kayaker capsizes and then rights the boat without getting out of it. There are several kinds of rolls. Kayakers today call these moves Eskimo rolls. Inuit hunters who rolled wore watertight jackets that fastened directly to the rims of the holes in their kayaks. This allowed them to roll into the icy Arctic without getting water in their boats.

Not all Inuit kayakers rolled their kayaks, but in some places, the combination of rough water and dangerous hunting made rolling necessary. For kayakers in these regions, rolling was an important skill. Sometimes, during a hunt, a harpoon line could tangle and capsize a boat. Sometimes an injured animal attacked a hunter and tipped the

This diagram illustrates the basics of an Eskimo roll, which is still an essential skill for many kayakers today. Paddlers who capsize use their hips to return to an upright position.

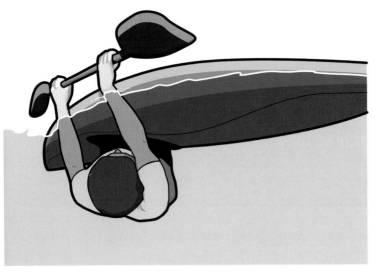

boat over. The kayaker needed to be able to roll the boat back up. The Greenland Inuit were masters of the roll. They paddled narrow kayaks in tricky waters and developed many types of rolls. They could roll their boats using their paddles, their harpoon shafts, or just their hands.

TRADITIONAL KAYAKING TODAY

Today, many of the skills of traditional kayaking have been lost. Modern advances and manufactured goods make kayaking less necessary to Inuit life. In addition, many of the animals the Inuit hunted have been overhunted and are now endangered. The kayak, the "hunter's boat," can no longer serve its original purpose.

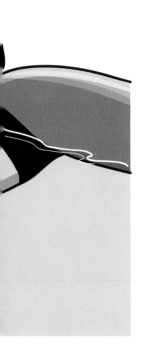

Despite that, however, kayaking has been given new life as a sport and cultural pursuit. Qaannat Kattuffiat—or, the Greenland Kayak Association—was started in 1985 to introduce new generations of kayakers to kayaking as it was traditionally practiced. Clubs around Greenland teach traditional kayak building and other skills. Traditional kayaking competitions are also held annually. The influence of this movement is not limited to Greenland either—a U.S. chapter has helped Americans learn and appreciate ancient kayaking as an important cultural form.

Kayak design and the materials used in the building of kayaks evolved over time, as kayaking began to appeal to casual adventurers. "Foldaboats," or collapsible kayaks, made their first appearance at the Olympics in 1936. In the 1950s, rigid, fiberglass boats became standard due to the superior lightness, strength, and durability of fiberglass. In the 1980s boat makers introduced the plastic kayak, fondly referred to by boaters as "Tupperware" and very difficult to damage. Even if they opt for the fiberglass, plastic, or other modern materials of today, however, professional and recreational kayakers all over the world today share much—and owe much—to the many preceding generations of Inuit kayakers.

CHAPTER 2

THE ESSENTIALS OF KAYAKING

G etting the right gear is the first step to starting any outdoor activity, and kayaking is no exception. Knowing what you're looking for and understanding the basic mechanics of the equipment you'll be handling is an important part of any kayaking experience. Naturally, a boat and paddle are always required. You should also always have a personal flotation device (PFD) and spray skirt. If you're planning on whitewater kayaking, a helmet is required as well. There are other recommended items, but these are the essentials.

THE VESSEL

First things first: the boat. All kayaks are basically the same. The hull of a kayak is a closed tube with a pointed bow and stern. The boat is slightly wider than a person's hips and the main opening is a hole in the middle of the top for the kayaker to shimmy into.

The two major sub-groups of kayaks are sea kayaks and whitewater kayaks. The sea kayak is a long, stable boat designed for lakes, quiet rivers, and ocean touring. The whitewater kayak is smaller and shorter. It fits your body more tightly and turns very easily. The whitewater kayak allows its more fearless paddlers (or wearers) to perform wild aquabatics in crashing river rapids. The extreme end of this spectrum is the "squirt boat." Even shorter and smaller than the whitewater kayak, the squirt boat can "squirt" forth—sometimes in a controlled spin and

Sea kayaks such as these are long and narrow. Their design keeps them stable in lakes, oceans, and even slow-moving rivers.

sometimes in a total panic—from the black depths of the most dangerous rapids. Squirt boats can even become vertical or be used to perform a number of other tricks.

FACTORS TO CONSIDER

Rather than buying a boat immediately, it is a good idea to rent and borrow as many types and brands as possible. This will help you develop a feel for what you like the best. There are some basic guidelines: larger, longer boats are harder to capsize and are faster for straight-ahead travel. Smaller boats are less stable but are more maneuverable and a better bet for the trickier bits of river runs.

It is also a good idea to look at a lot of boats closely and to start to understand how shape affects performance. In addition to size and length, stability is also due to "rocker." Rocker is the amount of curve along the keel. Touring kayaks have flatter keels. This helps keep them going in one direction. Whitewater boats have more rocker, or curve, to their keels. The bow and stern of a whitewater kayak are, on average, six inches higher than the part of the hull in the middle of the boat beneath the seated kayaker. This makes it much easier to turn.

Picture the raised ends of the boat skidding right or left across the surface of the water, rather than plowing through it underneath the surface. This is very useful when you are trying to avoid a huge boulder looming up in the middle of a fast-moving river. The downside is that the more rocker a boat has, and the easier it is to turn, the less stable it is.

Stability is also affected by "flare" and "chine." Flare refers to the amount that the sides of a kayak angle outward. If you cut a piece-

Whitewater kayaks are shorter than sea kayaks. They are designed to turn more easily in rapids, which allows kayakers to quickly dodge rocks and other obstacles they come across.

of-bread slice or cross-section out of the middle of a kayak, it would look more or less oval. The cross-sections of some kayaks flare so that they look wider at the top where they touch the waterline. The more flare a boat has, the more stable it is. Chine refers to the angle between the bottom of a boat and its sides. If the cross-section of a boat is more oval, it has a "soft chine." If it is more of a right angle, it has a "hard chine." The more chine a boat has, the more stable it is.

Whitewater kayaks generally have little or no flare or chine. They are very easy to capsize but also very easy to roll back up. Sea kayaks have both flare and chine and tend to keep their paddlers dryer.

HOW TO CHOOSE A BOAT

Before you make a final decision about which kayak to buy, you should think about where you want to kayak, how often you want to kayak, and how long you plan on being on the water. The material and size you choose will depend on how you plan to use the kayak. Think about the following questions before you make the leap into a purchase:

1. Where are you planning to kayak? Decide if you want to be on calm waters or whitewater, in large bodies of water or more shallow rivers and creeks. The answer may be some combination of all. Some boats are better suited to certain types of water than others.
2. Do you want to kayak regularly or just on occasion recreationally?
3. Are you planning on being on the water for hours at a time or covering several miles at a stretch? Would you like to do trips over several days or weeks?
4. How many people will be kayaking with you? Do you want a shared kayak or will you each have your own boat?

Most sea kayaks are made of fiberglass or plastic. The overall best bet, looking at cost, weight, and durability, is probably plastic.

Portaging with a partner is less strenuous than portaging alone. However, be sure to communicate with each other to coordinate your movements and avoid obstacles.

Plastic boats are nearly indestructible. Plastic is relatively inexpensive and comes in a range of styles. It is heavy (it weighs about ten percent more than fiberglass) but if you plan to spend all your time in the water, weight doesn't matter. If you plan to do a lot of "portaging"—carrying your boat overland from one water site to another—weight will be a larger part of your decision.

If you are willing to spend a bit more, fiberglass boats are far more beautiful than plastic ones, and they make less noise in the water. This may not matter in crashing rapids, but it is lovely to glide through a silent inlet in a fiberglass kayak. Fiberglass also needs more mainte-

ENVIRONMENTAL STEWARDSHIP

One of the great benefits of kayaking is that it allows you to observe and experience many of nature's wonders firsthand. As you begin your own paddling pursuits, it is important to consider your impact on the lakes, oceans, rivers, canyons, and all the surrounding areas you encounter. Preserving the beauty and health of these regions means the continued survival of the wildlife that depends on these areas as well as the continued enjoyment of all the paddlers, hikers, and others who journey there.

Environmental stewardship an important goal that requires the cooperation of many different parties. Basic tips for kayakers include taking all your litter back with you and disposing of it in a designated trash receptacle, avoiding dragging your kayak over vegetation on banks and shores, and steering clear of areas where local wildlife might nest, feed, or live. Organizations such as Leave No Trace and American Whitewater help educate those who enjoy nature on outdoor ethics and how they can minimize any negative effects their actions may have on the environment. These organizations and others like them, often partner with paddling groups in a joint effort to preserve natural resources—such as waterways for kayakers—and ensure that all individuals who enjoy nature share responsibility in protecting it.

nance. It can tear and, if you paddle in saltwater, you will need to hose your boat down afterward to clean off any salty residue.

If you are a whitewater kayaker, you will find that nowadays—except for in the case of very specialized squirt boats—almost all whitewater kayaks are plastic. If your primary interest is in running rivers, you will want a general-purpose plastic river boat. If you are more interested in doing stunts and routines, you may need a more specialized "rodeo" playboat.

CHOOSING A PADDLE

Now that you have a boat, you need a paddle. Choosing the right paddle is almost as important as choosing the right boat, but it is a much less expensive decision. In fact, like a lot of people, you may want a second, emergency paddle that is completely different from your main paddle.

The Inuit developed the double-bladed kayaking paddle—one shaft or handle with a paddle blade at each end—so they could paddle continuously, without having to switch sides in the boat. There have been several changes to paddle construction since the Inuit days, but the main features of a good paddle are still weight, strength, and balance.

One post-Inuit advance is "feathering." A feathered paddle has angled blades; as you hold one blade flat and look along the shaft, the other is anywhere from a few degrees slanted to fully vertical. When you stroke with a feathered paddle, as one blade pulls through the water, the other slices edge-forward through the air and knifes back into the water as your motion twists the shaft. This

It is helpful to try different types of paddles before you make a final decision about purchasing one.

is marvelous in strong wind, when the flat side of an unfeathered paddle can catch the air like a sail.

There are numerous small, personal choices about paddles. Paddle blades are either flat or curved like a spoon. Flat blades are convenient because you can paddle with either side. Spooned blades grab the water better and move through it faster. Large blades push against more water; smaller blades offer more control. Oval paddle shafts fit nicely in your hands and force you to hold the paddle correctly. A round shaft allows you to rotate the paddle more easily.

Wooden paddles are traditional and beautiful; wooden shafts have a nice, flexible give and never get deathly cold. However, they tend to be expensive, and they demand extra care. If you don't mind doing without looks and warmth, fiberglass is durable, less expensive, and flexible. Carbon fiber, Kevlar, and graphite are light and durable. However, they can be very expensive, and for casual kayaking, another material might be more practical.

Some paddles are made in two pieces. This means you can take them apart to store them. You can also change the amount of feather when you put them back together. Paddlers often choose to use take-apart paddles as their spares. They bungee-cord them in two pieces to the decks of their sea kayaks or store them underneath the deck of whitewater boats.

Choose your paddle length according to your height, the length of your arms, the type of boat you have, and how you paddle it. You will want a shorter shaft and narrower blades for fast, whitewater paddling, and a longer shaft and more generously sized blades for long trips across wide stretches of flat water. Try as many types and shapes as you can before you make a decision. Remember, there is nothing more exhausting than battling with a too-long paddle in too-strong wind at the end of a long day.

SAFETY FIRST

No matter how well you swim, no matter how warm the water, no matter how short the distance from your kayak to the shore, you will need a life jacket.

Unlike the orange neck pillows you may remember hating, the kayaker's personal flotation device or PFD is actually a cool

A PFD is necessary even when you are kayaking on quiet waters. Different styles are available to suit your particular needs, so it is worth investigating the options.

piece of boating gear. Its short cut allows the kayaker to twist freely at the waist. Different designs are available for males and females, and PFDs come in every imaginable color. Pick the one you like, but remember that safety is more important than appearance or comfort. Many also have pockets you can use to store your various personal items.

When you buckle on a good PFD it will feel secure around your body and not threaten to rise over your head. Do up every buckle, zipper, and waist tie and tighten them; if you leave it open in the front, it won't work. When you do take it off at the beach to eat lunch, tie it down. The last thing you—or your traveling companions—want is to have to hike out from the middle of a fantastic river because you've lost your PFD to a sudden wind.

STAYING DRY

The spray skirt is what makes your boat a true kayak. It is the piece of coated nylon or neoprene that keeps waves from spilling over your coaming—the curved lip around the edge of the cockpit—into the inside of your boat. It keeps you dry if you capsize, and it allows you to perform an Eskimo roll, which is how you roll your boat back upright from an upside-down position without getting out. The spray skirt also keeps you warm.

Nylon spray skirts are moderately priced and are good for moderate conditions. Neoprene skirts are more expensive and more watertight. They will keep you warmer in the cold but can make you feel far too hot in summer heat. If you plan to kayak in cold weather, you should take into account the extra thickness of winter clothes when you measure yourself for a spray skirt. Generally, though, tighter is better. No one likes cold water seeping down into the cockpit. If you plan to roll frequently, you will need a spray skirt designed to handle rough conditions. The grab loop of the spray skirt should be accessible at all times so that you can detach it from the coaming when needed. Also remember to put on your PFD *after* you attach the spray skirt. This ensures that the skirt fits the boat more tightly.

Now you've got the basics: a boat, a paddle, a personal flotation device (PFD), and a spray skirt. Before you set out, however, there are a few more pieces of equipment you may want to consider.

CHAPTER 3

ADDITIONAL EQUIPMENT

There are numerous items that aren't necessarily required for a kayaking experience but can be incredibly useful if you veer off course, damage your boat, hurt yourself, or are kayaking for long stretches of time. Some strongly recommended items include waterproof packing and flotation bags, a rope bag, bilge pumps, paddle floats, wetsuits, drysuits, sea socks, weather radios, compasses, maps, a global positioning system (GPS), knives, cell phones, flashlights, and emergency signaling devices. For those interested in taking in some sights, bring binoculars or a camera along, too.

Although breaking a paddle is rare, you will need a spare paddle. Not having a spare can be a disaster. Even if you never capsize, you may lose a paddle to a campsite flood or, if it's wooden, to an obnoxious beaver. A take-apart model is easy to strap to your deck or slide behind your seat. Getting a spare paddle is a good opportunity to pick a paddle of different length or blade size from your main paddle.

Ocean boaters might also consider a paddle leash made from thin nylon line or elastic cord that connects your paddle either to your wrist or to the deck of your boat. Another paddle accessory is a drip ring. Drip rings are rubber rings that slide onto the shaft of your paddle and prevent water from running down the shaft onto your hands and arms. A paddle float is an inflatable bag that fits onto the blade of your paddle. If you capsize and exit the boat, you can inflate the paddle float, attach it to your paddle, and use the combination as a float to support your climb

Paddle floats are especially useful tools for kayakers who capsize, perform a wet exit, and need to reenter their boats.

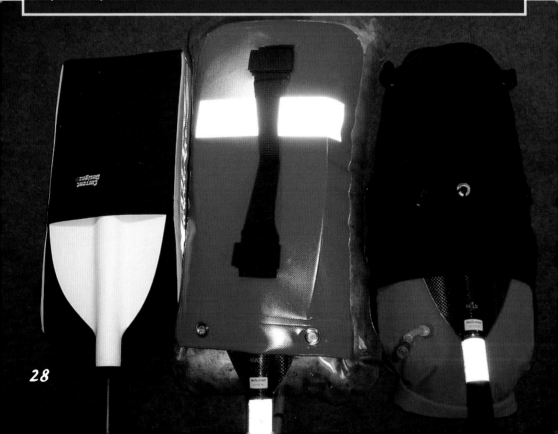

back into the boat. Paddle floats are effective, easy to stow, quite inexpensive, and essential, especially for anyone kayaking alone and away from others.

You may also want a bilge pump. If you plan to paddle solo far from land on the open sea, you will need one. Bilge pumps bail the water out of a righted or swamped boat. They can be electric or manual; the electric ones are fast, heavy, expensive, and do all the work for you. The handheld, manual pumps are light, inexpensive, require some elbow grease, and are more appropriate for kayaks.

FLOTATION

Kayaks need flotation at both ends. Sea kayaks have built-in compartments or bulkheads in the bow and stern where boaters store camping gear or lunch. Others use air bags in front of the feet and behind the seat. Flotation is particularly important in a boat loaded down with camping equipment.

For long, open crossings on lakes or oceans, boaters without bulkheads often use sea socks. These are large, coated nylon bags that fit into the hull and tie around the coaming. You sit inside the sock inside the kayak and secure your spray skirt on the coaming over it. A sea sock doesn't provide the buoyancy of bulkheads or air bags, but it does reduce the amount of water that can come on board if you capsize.

If you plan to do anything longer than a day trip, you will need nylon or vinyl waterproof dry bags to store gear in your boat. These are not flotation bags, but they do aid buoyancy because the more space they take up—crammed full of food and equipment—the less space there is for water to fill when you capsize. Nylon is lighter, easier to pack, less apt to tear, and doesn't stiffen in cold weather. Vinyl is less expensive. Dry bags are usually referred to by color and size. "Hey, grab Big Red, will you?" or "Toss on over Little Yellow."

TECH AND TOOLS

There is a wide variety of technology and tools that you can bring with you when kayaking that can help you along the way. Anything that is not waterproof will require a waterproof storage case or dry bag. There are many types of hard and soft cases available in

Although not as high tech as a GPS device or smartphone, a handheld compass is useful in areas where cell coverage is poor or when another device needs charging.

different sizes to suit your particular needs. These are especially useful if you decide to bring expensive items, such as cell phones, cameras, and GPS devices, with you.

One of the most important things to consider when embarking on a wilderness adventure is how not to get lost. Rivers generally make it hard to lose your way, but sea and lake kayakers should carry a compass, a device that magnetically determines geographical direction. Small, inexpensive, hiking compasses are perfectly adequate if you know how to use them. (Using a compass may be trickier than you think; talk to your kayaking instructor or someone at the sporting goods store before embarking on your trip.) There are also big, heavy, waterproof marine compasses that attach to your boat and provide readings of the direction of your bow.

Much cooler than a compass—and a bit more expensive—is the global positioning system, or GPS. This is a small, handheld device that triangulates your position by satellite. You can use it to pinpoint your position anywhere on earth to within about a hundred yards. It is particularly useful in fog, on overcast nights, or for long, open crossings where boaters have to take compass readings almost constantly.

Of course, most smartphones are able to serve as navigation aids as well. With the right apps, you can use your phone to pinpoint your location, track your route, geo-tag your photos and videos, share your trip on social media, check flow rates of the water, and more.

There may be some advantages to using a handheld GPS instead of or in addition to a smartphone. Namely, some GPS units are waterproof, need to be charged less frequently than a cell phone, do not need to be in a provider's coverage area to function, and don't require a data plan or phone connection to download maps.

If taking in the sights or documenting your trip are on your agenda, you might also want to consider two other items: a camera and binoculars. Again, a smartphone with a camera may also serve your needs, but a waterproof camera can withstand moisture better than most cell phones and is generally easier to replace in case it is dropped or becomes damaged. Binoculars are great for zooming in on distant wildlife or other sights you pass along the way. More serious observers can invest in expensive camera equipment or binoculars, but inexpensive options are available for the casual tourist, too.

STAYING SAFE

Unless you are perfecting your Eskimo roll in a swimming pool, or paddling within shouting distance of the Coast Guard, you will need some emergency signaling devices. The most basic is a flare, which produces a bright light for signaling. There are several kinds of flares. Meteor flares send a rocket up several hundred feet and continue to burn while they fall. Parachute flares use a small parachute to keep the light aloft. Handheld flares are useful on flat, open water and last for about two minutes.

You can also purchase a strobe light or a signal mirror. Strobe lights are battery-powered and highly visible by day and night. They can also be tested, unlike flares, and can be turned off to save power when no rescuer is in sight. In sunny weather, nothing catches the eye of a search and rescue pilot like the flash of a single mirror.

UNIVERSAL RIVER SIGNALS

Knowing the commonly understood river signals is a critical part of water safety. A river is a loud and complicated place. When you cannot make yourself heard above the roar of the whitewater, you will quickly see the value of knowing how to talk with your paddle or arms.

Emergency/Warning/Help Signal: Wave your paddle, helmet, or PFD over your head from side to side. If you use your paddle, hold it vertically.

Stop: Tell other paddlers to stop by raising your paddle horizontally above your head, or sticking out your arms straight out horizontally to your sides.

I'm OK: If you want your worried fellow paddlers to know you are okay, raise your open hand above your head and pat yourself on the helmet.

Proceed Straight: If everything is fine, and you want the paddlers behind to follow you straight down the middle of the river, hold your paddle straight above your head with its face toward them.

Proceed This Direction: If everything is fine, and you want the paddlers behind to follow you to one side or the other, angle your paddle 45° toward the desired route.

Remember: Never, ever point toward an obstacle or the people watching you will kayak straight into it.

A major piece of safety equipment for the whitewater kayaker is the throw rope. A throw rope enables you to pull another struggling or capsized kayaker out of a tricky place in a river. It is important to learn how to use a throw rope correctly from an instructor or advanced boater. If you throw a rope without bracing (supporting) it, you may be pulled into a dangerous river by the kayaker you are trying to save. If you brace it incorrectly around your arm or leg, you may cut off your own circulation. Once you do know how to use a throw rope, you should carry it with you whenever you are scouting rapids from a river bank. You never know when a friend or stranger may need your help.

Keeping a first aid kit for emergencies is strongly recommended. Drinking water—about a gallon per person—is also important, especially in very warm weather.

HOW TO DRESS

The number one choice in cold-weather, watersport garb for surfers, scuba divers, sailors, and kayakers is the drysuit. A drysuit is a tight-fitting suit that will actually keep you completely dry from neck to wrists to ankles even when fully submerged in ice-cold water. The drawback is that it can be constricting to wear one in a kayak. River boaters tend to wear dry tops, which keep them dry and warm from the waist up while their legs stay warm beneath their kayak skirts.

The next choice is the wetsuit. A wetsuit—like the sturdier spray skirts—is made of neoprene. It fits snugly against your body but is not watertight. When you capsize, it traps a thin film of water against your skin. Warmed by your body heat, this layer of water becomes an incredibly effective layer of insulation. Wetsuits range from neck-to-wrist-to-ankle outfits to vest tops and shorts. Kayakers wear sleeveless "farmer John" versions that allow them full freedom to move their arms.

If you don't plan to kayak in cold spring water (or you hate to shop) you may already own everything you need. Desirable materials include wool and synthetics like lycra or polypropylene. Water runs right out of these fabrics, and they keep you warm even when they're wet. Cotton T-shirts are not good because they hold water rather than draining it off—if you've ever been pushed into a pool you may have noticed this.

Wetsuits come in many different styles for different weather conditions and body types. If you opt for your own clothing, choose fabrics that are waterproof and keep you warm.

It is always wise to layer. If you buy only one kayak-specific piece of clothing, you might pick a paddling jacket or loose pull-over of treated nylon. Unlike the average windbreaker, paddling jackets are designed with neoprene closures at the neck and wrists to keep out the water.

You might also want to consider buying paddling gloves, because wet skin blisters easily. For cold weather, you can wear pogies, special mittens that attach to the shaft of your paddle. You will definitely need thick-soled sneakers or nylon sandals to protect your feet from rocky lake and river bottoms. (Remember: when spilled into fast-moving water, keep your feet up and pointed downstream and let your rubber soles and backside bump off the rocks. Never stand in moving water; you might catch your foot between two rocks and break your leg.)

PACE YOURSELF

Although it is important to have safe, high-quality equipment, there's no need to go crazy right up front. Before you jump into major purchases, take some time to learn the basics. This will help you discover what you like and don't like and determine how much you want to invest in your hobby. If you want to pursue kayaking as a long-term activity, you can slowly build up your collection of gear and equipment.

CHAPTER 4

GET PADDLING

Although by now you might be feeling more comfortable with the gear and equipment you need, you'll need to find a qualified paddling instructor before venturing out on your own. A quick lesson might be enough if you're planning on doing a scenic tour on calm waters, but if you're planning on kayaking regularly, an experienced paddler will teach you the right skills safely and in the right order. Such instruction will prevent you from developing bad habits. Trained instructors can also help you safely navigate tricky waters when you first set out and can answer questions as they arise. Books and online videos are useful in your preparation, but it is dangerous to go out on the water and teach yourself how to kayak without any in-person instruction.

There are many places that offer kayaking instruction. Local colleges, youth groups, or organizations such as the YMCA may offer lessons for younger or beginner students. An increasing

Books and videos are not enough for beginners. In-person instruction allows trained professionals to work with you one-on-one and zero in on your individual needs.

number of urban areas have also created whitewater parks, which feature manmade waterways or modified natural waterways at varying levels of difficulty. Some of these parks offer lessons and different courses beginners can try.

TAKING A SEAT

First—obviously!—you have to get into the boat. Make sure you're already wearing your PFD. Then step into your spray skirt while still on dry land, pull it up above your waist, and roll it up a little so it doesn't interfere with your legs. The most important thing to remember when climbing into any boat is to keep your weight low. Put your kayak into shallow water, grip your paddle shaft in one hand and press it flat across the rear of the cockpit. Use your other hand to hold the shaft just beyond the side of the boat with one blade resting on the shore for support. The even pressure from your hands should hold the boat steady. Step into the middle of the cockpit with one foot, sit carefully on the back deck, and pull in the other foot. Now, with your arms still behind you, slide over the paddle and down into the cockpit.

As your weight drops from waist-height to ankle-height, the boat will suddenly feel much more secure. Now bring your paddle around, balance it across the front deck and secure your spray skirt. It is generally easiest to start in the back, then attach the front, and finish with the sides. You will now feel very cozy. You may also be worried about ever getting out of this thing in the terrifying event of a capsize. Fortunately, there is a grab loop at the front of the skirt. Try pulling it forward and up and then toward you. Instantly the whole thing will release.

More than anything, you should feel that you are wearing the kayak. It should fit you like a good pair of jeans: not tight, but snug, and able to move with you as smoothly as part of your own body. When you are in your kayak, you should check the fit for your feet, knees, thighs, seat, back, and hips. Your feet will rest against a pair of pedals or a flat platform that adjusts to your height. A pair of padded braces holds your knees and thighs, and the seat, backrest, and foam hip pads should hold your body firmly without cramping your movement.

GETTING THE HANG OF IT

So here you are, wrapped in your kayak and ready to go. Time to pick up the paddle. Each of your hands has a slightly different job. Your main hand—the left for lefties and right for righties—is your "control" hand. The other is your "slip" hand. With your control hand, hold the paddle shaft about a fist's width from the top of the blade. Keep your wrist straight and pull the blade through the water. As it rises behind you, stroke down with your slip hand. Your control hand should always be firm on the paddle. Your slip hand should loosen between strokes so you can rotate the paddle and face the blade squarely to the water.

The correct motion here is box-like: first cock one wrist back by your shoulder, punch out with the paddle, and then stroke down and back. Concentrate on pushing the shaft out with your upper hand, rather than pulling back with the lower hand. One of the beauties of the double-bladed paddle is that you can use this stronger pushing force directly from your shoulder to power the boat.

Your instructor may start you off by standing beside your boat in calm, waist-deep water. To get a feel for the way the boat rests in the water, he or she may suggest you rock the boat from side to side. It is very important to be able to feel loose in the kayak and let it rock under you. The looser you are at the waist, the more stable and secure your kayak will feel. Your instructor will help you to hold the boat down to the right for a few seconds and then bring it upright with a snap of your hips. This hip-snap is the basis for the Eskimo roll.

It is common for beginners to practice wet exits and rolls in swimming pools because they are usually easier to access than natural bodies of water.

You may also try a wet exit. A wet exit is when you slide out of your capsized boat underwater. First you have to capsize. Before you tip over, make sure there are no rocks under you. Now, hold onto your paddle and throw your weight to one side of the boat until you pull it over. (This is called turtling the boat, because the upturned hull looks like the shell of a turtle.)

You are now hanging upside down from your boat in the water. Slide your control hand to the middle of your paddle. Use your slip hand to pull the grab loop on your skirt. When it comes free, grip the sides of the cockpit with your hands (your control hand is still holding the paddle) push back and away from the boat, and

Sea kayakers generally won't rely on bracing as much as whitewater kayakers but both types of kayaking require all of the same strokes.

somersault out of the boat. Your PFD will bring you to the surface.

The first time you do this, your instructor will probably let you tow your boat to shore and get back in the easy way. However, you do need to learn how to right your boat and get back in from the water—with or without help.

HOW TO PADDLE

Now that you are prepared for the worst, it's time to learn to enjoy yourself. First you need to learn how to paddle. Paddling breaks down into four major types of strokes. Although these blend to the untrained eye, they are quite distinct and have particular uses. The power stroke pulls you forward. The forward sweep pushes the boat forward and turns it away from the paddle side. The reverse sweep pushes the boat back and turns it away from the paddle side. The draw pulls the boat toward the paddle.

Sea kayakers and whitewater kayakers both use all of these strokes. However, touring is mainly about paddling, or moving the boat through still water, while river kayaking is also about keeping the boat stable in moving water. In order to hold a whitewater kayak stable in "squirrelly" water, you need to learn to brace. Bracing is a technique for holding a paddle in the water to stabilize a kayak.

There are low braces and high braces. In the low brace, you hold yourself and your kayak upright by rotating your wrists down and pressing the backside of the paddle onto the water. Just like when

PLAYING STICK AND PADDLING SWEEP

One way to test the speed and direction of whitewater is to toss sticks into it and make sure they "live." As a result, the kayaker who braves the first run describes her job as "playing stick." Usually one of the two most experienced kayakers on a trip plays stick, while the other most experienced paddler "sweeps." This means he or she brings up the rear and keeps counting heads to make sure no one gets left behind.

Beyond including a strong first and last paddler, every kayaking trip should have a clear group rescue plan. Every member of the trip should have some basic rescue skills, understand how to use a throw rope, and know the basics for getting to swimmers. Getting to swimmers quickly is probably the most important part of keeping a kayaking outing safe.

you bellyflop and smack against the hard surface of the pool, your paddle will resist sinking into the water. In this way, you can use the surface of the water to stabilize yourself.

In the high brace, you raise your arms, stick your paddle down into the water, and press the paddle face against a flat surface of water underwater. The high brace feels less secure than the low brace because lifting your arm so high raises your center of gravity (this is why the boat feels less stable when you stand). It is also dangerous because it can put enough pressure on your arms to dislocate your shoulder. The high brace is most useful when your boat is already tipped way over. It is generally considered an emergency brace. You should use the much safer low brace to try to prevent these emergencies.

LEARNING TO ROLL

If you catch on quickly and express an interest, perhaps you'll move right into the Eskimo roll. After all, you have already mastered the basic elements: the high and low brace and a gentle version of the hip snap.

Your need for a foolproof roll will vary with the type of kayaking you do. Many sea and lake kayakers never roll at all. On the other hand, there are unplanned situations in which a roll will save even the most cautious kayaker from a cold or dangerous swim. River wisdom dictates that, once over, you should "roll till you puke," to avoid that swim.

A successful Eskimo roll depends upon the power of the hips. To practice, paddle your kayak into waist-deep water at the lip of a pool or next to a friend or instructor. Lean over and hold the pool edge or person's hands. Flip yourself and your boat until you are as close to upside down as you can get with your cheek just resting on the surface of the water so you can breathe. Now, focus all your strength into your hips.

The hip snap flicks your body like a whip. Power moves up from your hips and along your side and yanks your shoulders, neck, and head out of the water—but only after the boat is righted. A strong whip curves like an arch. If you try to pull your head up first—which is tempting because you want to breathe—the whip shape will collapse and your boat will re-turtle. This is because your hip

A successful Eskimo roll depends on your hip control and ability to snap yourself back upright.

muscles are strong enough to lift your head but your neck muscles cannot lift your whole body and your kayak. It is best to practice this motion many times. Keep turtling and righting your boat over and over while keeping your cheek resting, unmoving, on the surface of the pool. This motion will also teach you to keep your waist loose, which lets the kayak ride out bumps on the river and keeps it much more stable.

Most kayakers use the screw roll as their basic (or combat) roll. The other basic survival roll is called the C-to-C. Whichever you prefer, it is important to have a totally reliable roll that will get you up even "in traffic"—which means no matter how rough or complicated the water is around you.

KEEP ON ROLLING

Once your hip snap is perfect, you will be able to learn to hand roll. In a hand roll, you substitute the motion of your hand for the motion of your paddle and pull the boat around almost entirely with your body. Hand rolling is more than a stunt. Kayak-polo players often lose their paddles and capsize when shooting goals. On rough rivers a kayaker in trouble can sometimes use a hand roll to reach the bank or retrieve a dropped paddle.

Perfecting your screw roll is about as exciting as it gets in a swimming pool. However, once you get the hang of these basics, you'll be ready to hit the real outdoors. Few things compare to the thrill of kayaking in nature, whether you choose a lake, ocean, or rapid. Some of the world's most breathtaking sights can be viewed from the cockpit of a kayak.

CHAPTER 5

YOUR ADVENTURE AWAITS

Once you've completed the necessary preparation, you'll be ready to experience kayaking as it was meant to be done—in the great outdoors. A local lake or nearby ocean is a good place to start, if either of those is available to you. A flat, slow-moving section of river may also be a good beginner's spot. Whitewater parks and state and national parks often offer recreational boating options for people with or without their own equipment. Look online or ask your parents for suggested practice locations if you can't immediately find a local kayaking destination.

GETTING STARTED OUTDOORS

Guided kayak tours are a great way to get a feel for some kayaking basics in nature without having to invest in much equipment or

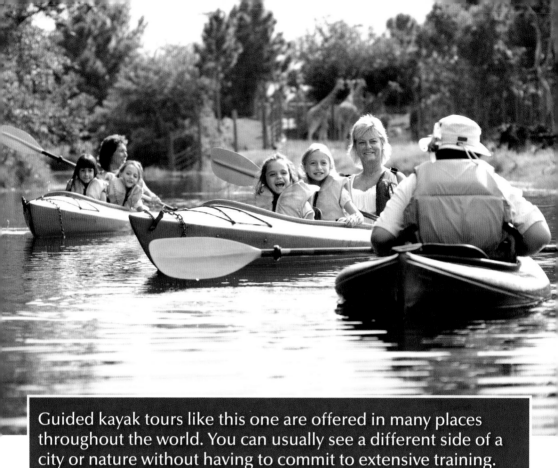

Guided kayak tours like this one are offered in many places throughout the world. You can usually see a different side of a city or nature without having to commit to extensive training.

training. You can usually observe wildlife and work in some exercise at a relaxed pace without spending hours perfecting a roll. You might also consider joining a local paddling club, through which you can meet fellow paddlers and have the opportunity to rent or borrow gear before buying your own.

As you become more comfortable, you can work your way up to more difficult rapids. Before you go, though, remember this: although there is always the opportunity to push yourself, this does not mean you should behave irresponsibly or attempt something that frightens you. Be sure to consult the International Scale of River Difficulty for any whitewater run you attempt.

THE INTERNATIONAL SCALE OF RIVER DIFFICULTY

While no two rivers are exactly the same, a rating system used to gauge the difficulty of the rapids in a particular area is very useful when deciding on a kayaking location that is suited to your skill level. This is the American version of the International Scale, according to the organization, American Whitewater. Regardless of how a location is classified, however, it is important to stay vigilant and use your best judgment—if weather, a fallen tree, or other variables look like they might present a problem, prepare accordingly.

Class I (pre-beginner) Class I water is fast and smooth with obvious obstructions that are easy to avoid. It poses little danger for swimmers, and spilled kayakers will not need assistance to recover themselves and their boats.

Class II (novice) Class II water is faster, includes more rocks and waves, but offers visually obvious routes and does not demand scouting from the banks. Swimmers are generally able to rescue themselves.

Class III (intermediate) Class III runs include rocks and ledges that require quick turns and maneuvers. Truly dangerous rocks or waves are avoidable, but the water demands good boat control. Inexperienced boaters should scout Class III water before running it. Party members should be prepared to offer help to swimmers.

continued on the next page

continued from the previous page

Class IV (advanced) Class IV water may include unavoidable holes, large waves, or narrow stretches between rocks and ledges. Kayakers may be forced to execute strong, fast turns to avoid obstructions or cross eddy lines. Boating parties need to scout Class IV sections before running them. Given the level of risk for swimmers, only kayakers with a practiced Eskimo roll should attempt these runs.

Class V (expert) Class V water is for experts. It includes long stretches of violent water, steep drops, and narrow, complex passages. The consistency of the difficulty requires both physical strength and endurance. Class V water must be scouted each time it is run, although it may include sections that are tricky to view from the bank. The risks for swimmers are significant.

Class VI (extreme and exploratory) Class VI runs push the envelope even for experts. They are technically challenging, unpredictable, and may never have been run before. The force of the water or sheer sides of the river canyon may make rescuing swimmers impossible.

COMPETITIONS

If you want to kayak competitively, there are three general categories of kayaking games. Each demands the capabilities of a boater at a strong intermediate level or better. The most grueling is the down-river slalom race. This type of race tends to be ten miles (sixteen kilometers) or more and requires highly developed river-reading skills as well as strong upper-body muscles. Your task is to choose the most efficient path through the course and finish in the shortest time.

Slalom-gate courses are short, usually about 50 yards (45.7 m) long, and comparable to slalom skiing courses in their use of "gates." The kayaker runs the gates—which occur among and around various tricky bits of whitewater—in a particular order that sometimes involves a fair amount of backpaddling. Contestants are judged for

Gates, such as the ones seen here, are spread throughout slalom courses to challenge advanced kayakers as they navigate difficult rapids.

Playboaters like the one seen here perform stunts only in certain types of water features called playspots.

time and lose points for missing or touching gates as well as for running them out of order. Slalom kayaking is one type of kayaking event featured in the summer Olympic games. It has been featured regularly since 1992. The other kayaking event in the Olympics is known as sprint kayaking. This event is more straightforward, with kayakers paddling in a straight line of a given distance (usually 200, 500, or 1,000 meters [656; 1,640; or 3,280 feet]) in a speed contest against other competitors.

The playboater's version of competitive kayaking is freestyle kayaking, or rodeo. A freestyle kayaking "course" (or playspot) is a water feature like the hole at the bottom of a drop. Sometimes a contest involves specific moves. Sometimes people use their imaginations—they do airborne somersaults or spin upside down or juggle fruit. Competitive playboating used to mean a bunch of very good stunt kayakers showing off; today it means complex and demanding moves linked into ballet-like routines.

The nice thing about kayaking is that there is plenty of room for many interest and skill levels, from sightseers to playboaters and everyone in between. However or wherever you choose to kayak, you are sure to discover some amazing aspects of both nature and yourself along the way.

GLOSSARY

BOW The front of a boat.

BRACE A technique for holding a paddle in the water to stabilize a kayak.

BULKHEAD A sealed compartment in the bow or stern of a kayak used for storage and flotation.

COAMING The curved lip around the edge of the cockpit.

DRAW A paddle stroke that pulls or pushes a boat sideways.

DROP A waterfall over which a kayaker drops from a smooth lip of water to a pool below.

EDDY The still or slow-moving area of water behind a protecting feature like a rock.

FEATHERING Positioning kayak paddle blades so that they are at opposite angles.

HIP-SNAP The strong, hip-first body jerk that allows paddlers to right their capsized kayaks; the basis for the Eskimo roll.

HOLE A circular water feature that can form behind an obstruction and submerge or trap a kayaker.

HULL The body of a boat.

INUIT A group of native peoples of the Arctic.

OBSTRUCTION A rock or other object that can block a paddler's path and cause rapids.

PLAYBOATING A type of whitewater kayaking in which kayakers perform stunts in a single location, or playspot

RAPIDS The foaming whitewater that forms around rocks and underwater obstructions or from contradictory currents.

ROLL The way a kayaker rights a kayak without getting out of it.

SQUIRRELLY Of or relating to water that moves in an irregular pattern.

STERN The back of a boat.

SWEEP A paddle stroke whose long bow-to-stern arc turns the boat away from the paddle side.

WHITEWATER Quickly moving water in a river that appears white because of the speed at which it travels over rocks.

American Whitewater
P.O. Box 1540
Cullowhee, NC 28723
(866) 262-8429
Website: https://www.americanwhitewater.org
Dedicated to preserving whitewater resources around the United States,
American Whitewater works with a variety of organizations, including conser-
vation and paddling groups as well as government agencies, to advocate and
provide resources to the public.

The American Canoe Association (ACA)
503 Sophia Street, Suite 100
Fredericksburg, VA 22401
(540) 907-4460
Website: https://aca.site-ym.com
The ACA serves individuals involved in various paddlesports, including canoeing,
rafting, and kayaking. The organization offers safety tips, instructional resources,
competition information, and more.

CanoeKayak Canada
700-2197 Riverside Drive
Ottawa, ON K1H 7X3
Canada
(613) 260-1818
Website: http://canoekayak.ca
CanoeKayak Canada is Canada's national body for competitive kayaking,
canoeing, and other paddlesports. The organization is responsible for national
paddling competitions and equips teams with coaches, equipment, and other
resources.

The Lincoln Street Kayak and Canoe Museum (LSKCM)
5340 S.E. Lincoln Street
Portland, OR 97215
(503) 234-0264
Website: http://www.traditionalkayaks.com/museum.html
Visitors to the LSKCM can view carefully constructed replicas of a wide variety of indigenous watercraft, including kayaks, and paddles from around the world, and learn more about their cultural and historical significance. All replicas are designed by artist Harvey Golden.

Paddle Canada
P.O. Box 126, Station Main
Kingston, ON K7L 4V6
Canada
(888) 252-6292, ext. 10
Website: http://www.paddlecanada.com
Paddle Canada is responsible for setting national standards in paddling for instruction and certification in Canada. In addition to instructor resources, the organization offers information to students on classes and various paddling programs.

Paddlesports North America (PNA)
124 W. Willow
Lansing, MI 48906
(515) 999-5762
Website: http://www.paddlesportsnorthamerica.org
PNA educates the public about paddlesports through resources on safety and environmental stewardship. Classroom and on-water training is also offered with lessons developed by British Canoeing.

Professional Paddlesports Assocation (PPA)
P.O. Box 10847
Knoxville, TN 37939
Website: http://propaddle.com
The PPA offers tips to those new to paddling, guiding them through choosing their craft, their gear, and their paddling destinations. Information on events, environmental stewardship, and more is also available.

Qajaq USA
American Chapter of the Greenland Kayak Association
Website: http://www.qajaqusa.org
Qajaq USA is dedicated to preserving the history and culture associated with traditional kayaking. As a chapter of the Greenland Kayak Association, members learn about traditional kayak building and techniques practiced by generations of kayakers in villages throughout Greenland.

WEBSITES

Because of the changing nature of Internet links, Rosen Publishing has developed an online list of websites related to the subject of this book. This site is updated regularly. Please use this link to access this list:

http://www.rosenlinks.com/OUT/Kayak

FOR FURTHER READING

Bigelow, Jodi. *Kayaking for Fitness: An 8-Week Program to Get Fit and Have Fun*. Beachburg, ON, Canada: The Heliconia Press, 2008.

Burnham, Bill, and Mary Burnham. *Kayaking for Everyone: Selecting Gear, Learning Strokes, and Planning Trips*. Guilford, CT: Morris Book Publishing, 2010.

Cunningham, Christopher. *Sea Kayaker's More Deep Trouble: More True Stories and Their Lessons*. Blacklick, OH: McGraw-Hill, 2014.

Dillon, Pamela S., and Jeremy Oyen, eds. *Kayaking*. Champaign, IL: Human Kinetics, 2009.

Dowd, John. *Sea Kayaking: The Classic Manual for Touring, from Day Trips to Major Expeditions*. New York, NY: Greystone Books, 2015.

Glickman, Joe. *Fearless: One Woman, One Kayak, One Continent*. Guilford, CT: Globe Pequot Press, 2012.

Johnson, Shelley. *The Complete Sea Kayaker's Handbook*. New York, NY: McGraw-Hill, 2011.

Loel, Collins. *Kayak Rolling: The Black Art Demystified*. Guilford, CT: Globe Pequot Press, 2009.

Matthews, Alex, and Ken Whiting. *Touring & Sea Kayaking: The Essential Skills and Safety*. Beachburg, ON, Canada: The Heliconia Press, 2012.

McGuffin, Gary, and Joanie McGuffin. *Paddle Your Own Kayak: An Illustrated Guide to the Art of Kayaking*. Erin, ON, Canada: Boston Mills Press, 2012.

Polley, Jason. *How to Survive Outdoors.* London, England: Teach Yourself, 2013.

Santella, Chris. *Fifty Places to Paddle Before You Die: Kayaking and Rafting Experts Share the World's Greatest Destinations.* New York, NY: Stewart, Tabori, and Chang, 2014.

Stuhaug, Dennis. *Kayaking Made Easy: A Manual for Beginners With Tips for the Experienced.* Guilford, CT: Globe Pequot Press, 2013.

Tyrrell, Diane. *101 Games and Activities for Canoes and Kayaks.* Monterey, CA: Healthy Learning, 2011.

Whiting, Ken. *Recreational Kayaking: The Ultimate Guide.* Beachburg, ON, Canada: The Heliconia Press, 2008.

Whiting, Ken, and Kevin Varette. *Whitewater Kayaking: The Ultimate Guide.* East Petersburg, PA: Fox Chapel Publishing, 2012.

INDEX

ABOUT THE AUTHORS

Serena J. Thomas is a writer who has enjoyed numerous kayaking tours around the United States as well as whitewater rafting trips in her native Sacramento County.

Allison Stark Draper is a writer and editor who grew up spending summers paddling on a lake in Maine. She lives in New York City and the Catskills.

PHOTO CREDITS

Cover, p. 1 Dragon Images/Shutterstock.com; p. 5 Blend Images – Michael DeYoung/Brand X Pictures/Getty Images; p. 7 Matthew M. Schoenfelder/Lonely Planet Images/Getty Images; p. 9 National Geographic/SuperStock; p. 10 Marilyn Angel Wynn/Nativestock/Getty Images; pp. 12-13 Dorling Kindersley/Getty Images; p. 16 Josh McCulloch/All Canada Photos/Getty Images; pp. 18, 35 Dennis Welsh/UpperCut Images/Getty Images; p. 20 sturti/E+/Getty Images; p. 23 © iStockphoto.com/sivarock; p. 25 Hero Images/Getty Images; p. 28 Mfranck/Wikimedia Commons/File:PaddleFloat.jpg/CC BY-SA 3.0; p. 30 Image Source/Getty Images; p. 38 Nick Daly/Cultura/Getty Images; p. 41 Will Salter/Lonely Planet Images/Getty Images; p. 42 filo/E+/Getty Images; p. 45 Danita Delimont/Gallo Images/Getty Images; p. 48 John Coletti/The Image Bank/Getty Images; p. 51 Chris Falkenstein/Stockbyte/Getty Images; p. 52 Charlie Munsey/Aurora/Getty Images; cover and interior pages Iwona Grodzka/iStock/Thinkstock (twig frame), AKIRA/amanaimagesRF/Thinkstock (wood frame)
Designer: Brian Garvey; Editor: Shalini Saxena;
Photo researcher: Nicole Baker